INFORMATION EXPLORER

SUPER SMART
INFORMATION
STRATEGIES

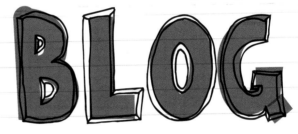

BLOG

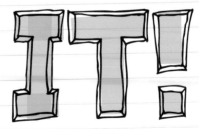

IT!

by Kristin Fontichiaro

CHERRY LAKE PUBLISHING • ANN ARBOR, MICHIGAN

CHAPTER ONE
Do You Need a Blog?

A blog is a great way to share exciting vacation stories.

Have you ever wanted to share everything you were doing on a family vacation with your friends back home? Have you ever wished you could give a sick classmate details about what was going on in school? Maybe you're helping your uncle fix up his classic car. If you could write about each step of the process, then people in the local car club could follow along.

If you like telling people what's happening, then you should think about starting a **blog**. A blog is a special kind of Web site where you can share your thoughts by writing **posts**. Blogging is kind of like writing in a journal or a diary. But most diaries or journals are about keeping your secrets private. Blogs are posted online for anyone to read. You can write every day, every few days, or when something special happens. Blogs let you include videos, photos, and sound recordings along with your words! Each time you add a new post to your blog, it appears at the very top of your Web page. This means that people who visit your blog always see the newest information first.

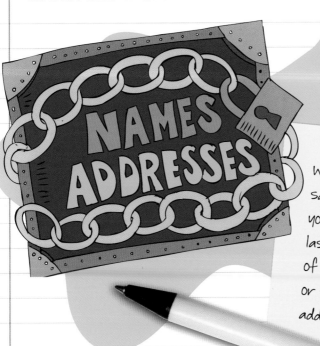

NAMES ADDRESSES

While the Web is almost always safe, keep your privacy in mind so you stay safe. Avoid using your last name as well as the full name of your friends, relatives, school, or sports team. Never give your address or phone number.

Blogs are a great way to let people know what you are doing, thinking about, and planning, right as it is happening. Some people write in the same blog for years and years. Your parents or guardians might keep a long-term blog with photos of you growing up.

Other blogs are kept just for a few months. Maybe your family is renovating your house. You can take turns adding photos and words to describe how the

Your blog could highlight the ways your house is improved during a renovation project.

Many teachers create blogs to keep their students up-to-date on homework assignments and other class news.

house changes each day. Maybe your sports team has a blog for the season. It might remind players when practices are, where the games will be held, and what happened during each game.

Some people use blogs in school. Your teacher might keep a blog to remind you of your homework. You and your classmates might take turns writing blog posts about class news.

There sure are a lot of things you can blog about!

TRY THIS!

What do you want to blog about? Brainstorm a list. Next to each topic, think about whether this is a long-term or short-term topic.

BRAINSTORM

Ask for permission from your parents or guardians before you start to blog. If you are at least 13 years old, you can set up your own blog. If you are not that old yet, ask your parents if they can set up a blog and share the password.

Possible Topics	How Long Would It Last?

To get a copy of this activity, visit www.cherrylakepublishing.com/activities.

CHAPTER TWO

Setting Up Your Blog

↖ Ask a parent or teacher to help you choose the blogging tools that are right for you.

There are lots of ways to set up a blog online for free.

1. If you have your own Web site, most **Web hosts** have blogging tools. You can install these on your site for no extra cost.

2. If you are blogging for a class project, your teacher might use a Web site such as Kidblog (*http://kidblog.org*). It sets up private blogs for each member of the class. You, your teacher, and your classmates can see it, but other people cannot. This is an excellent way to start blogging safely.

Blogger makes getting
started really easy!

3. If you are blogging for fun, you can use Google's
Blogger (*www.blogger.com*). Blogger is very
popular because it is free and easy to use. If
you have a Gmail account, you can use it to log
in to Blogger. If not, you'll need to create a new
account. You can set up as many blogs as you
want, but it's always easiest to start with one!
Blogger lets you post photos, **text**, and video.

4. The most powerful free blogging tool is
WordPress (*http://wordpress.com*). WordPress
lets you upload audio files. This is not possible
on Blogger. WordPress is more complicated than
most other blogging tools. You can **customize** it
much more, but Blogger and Kidblog are easier
for beginners to use.

Once you have an account at a blogging site, you need to choose a title for your blog. Sometimes people create titles that include their names, like Grace's Ideas or Jeff's Amazing Thoughts. Choose your title carefully to set a mood that is funny, thoughtful, or serious. Here are some examples of good blog titles:

- My Journey Through Fourth Grade
- Our Trip to the Grand Canyon
- Come to Our 2012 Block Party!
- Our Class Hamsters Are Growing!

A trip to the Grand Canyon would give you plenty of interesting things to blog about.

Be sure to pick a title that matches your topic. For example, I Love Mac and Cheese could be a great title for a food blog. But it would be a terrible title for a class newsletter! The good news is you can change your blog title at any time.

Now you need to create a **URL** for your blog. This is the address people will type in to visit your blog. If you are using Blogger, you need to think of something that will fit in this blank:

http://_____.blogspot.com

For WordPress, you need to fill in the blank here:

http://_____.wordpress.com

A food blog is a great way to share your experiences with cooking and eating delicious meals.

baby bunnies
little rabbits

Brainstorm a list
of possible URLs for your
blog, in case your first
choice isn't available.

Most people try to make their blog title and their
URL as similar as possible. You should brainstorm a
few backup possibilities, in case someone has already
taken the URL you want. No two Web sites can have
the same URL! Try to think of variations, such as 4th
instead of fourth, or rabbit instead of bunny. Or use
abbreviations, such as bc instead of Battle Creek. Use
lowercase letters only.

Let's look at the earlier title examples and give them some sample URLs:

Blog Title	Possible URLs
My Journey Through Fourth Grade	• http://fourthgrade.blogspot.com • http://4thgrade.wordpress.com • http://myjourneythroughfourthgrade.blogspot.com • http://4thgradejourney.wordpress.com
Our Trip to the Grand Canyon	• http://grandcanyontrip.wordpress.com • http://grandcanyontrip2012.blogspot.com • http://gcvacationjuly.wordpress.com
Come to Our 2012 Block Party!	• http://blockpartyinfo.blogspot.com • http://2012blockparty.blogspot.com • http://blockparty.wordpress.com
Our Class Hamsters Are Growing!	• http://ourhamsters.blogspot.com • http://hamstersgrowing.blogspot.com • http://room4hamsters.wordpress.com

When you are choosing your blog title or URL, don't give away personal information. That includes your last name and address.

Now that your blog has been created and named, you should customize its appearance. Every blogging site has many options you can choose from to change the look of your blog. These options are called **templates** or themes. They include different colors and illustrations that can help express your blog's mood, personality, or content. For example, a template with cupcakes on it would be perfect if you want to blog about your school's bake sale. But that same template might look weird if you were blogging about your trip to Niagara Falls!

Imagine you are at Niagara Falls. How would you describe it on your blog?

TRY THIS!

Come up with some possible subjects for your blog. Brainstorm a list of possible titles and URLs. Then think about what colors, images, or designs would be useful for those topics. Now, work with an adult to set up your blog account. Pick a title, URL, and theme.

To get a copy of this activity, visit www.cherrylakepublishing.com/activities.

Hello Bunny!

CHAPTER THREE

Writing Your First Post

You can outline your ideas on note paper before writing your blog posts.

Congratulations! Your blog is set up and ready to go. Now what do you want to post about?

Each blog post has two parts: a title and a **body**. The title is a lot like a newspaper headline. It should tell what the subject of the post will be. That way, people will know what to expect. The body is the main part of the post and contains your text, photos, videos, and more.

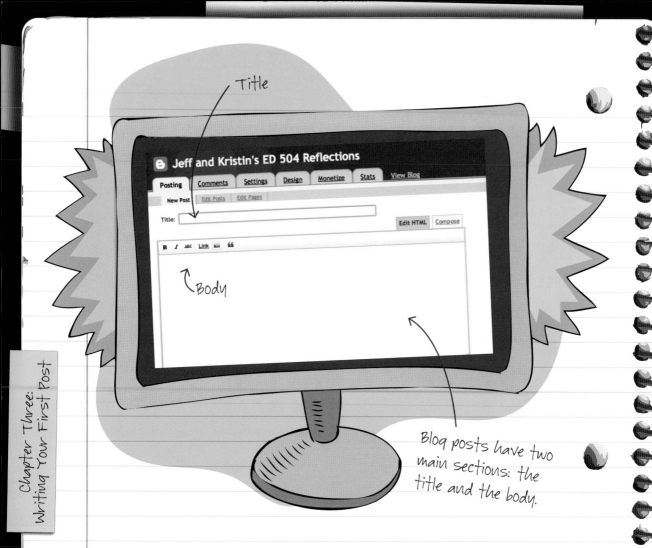

Title

Jeff and Kristin's ED 504 Reflections

Posting | Comments | Settings | Design | Monetize | Stats | View Blog

New Post | Edit Posts | Edit Pages

Title:

Edit HTML | Compose

B | I | ABC | Link | 66

Body

Blog posts have two main sections: the title and the body.

Most people use their first blog post to explain the purpose of the blog or the reason they are writing. Use a friendly, welcoming voice. If you want, you can add photos, audio, or video, too. Read the blog site's directions to find out how. Some people make a short outline or a list of things they want to say before they start writing. This helps them stay organized, especially if the blog post will be longer than a paragraph or two.

Let's look again at the four blog titles from chapter 2. Here are some examples of how you might begin writing those blogs.

Blog Title: My Journey Through Fourth Grade

Title of First Blog Post: Welcome to My Blog!

Body of First Post: Welcome to my blog! I'm Henry. In this blog, I'll tell you what it's like to be in fourth grade. I hope you will enjoy learning about my year!

Blog Title: Our Trip to the Grand Canyon

Title of First Blog Post: We're on Our Way!

Body of First Post: Our family is going to take a road trip all the way to the Grand Canyon! We'll be gone for two weeks, but we'll check in every day on this blog. We'll tell you what we saw, where we stopped, who we met, and what we did. We leave in fifteen minutes! Check out this video of Dad trying to jam one more suitcase into the trunk!

Blog Title: Come to Our 2012 Block Party!

Title of First Blog Post: Welcome to Our Planning Blog for Block Party 2012!

Body of First Post: Hi there, neighbors! If you live in the Vollintine-Evergreen Historic District, this blog is for you! We'll be blogging about all of our plans for our upcoming block party. Stay tuned. Each week, we'll give you an update on our plans. We hope you'll join us!

Blog Title: Our Class Hamsters Are Growing!

Title of First Blog Post: Meet the New Babies!

Body of First Post: On September 15, our class hamster had babies! Look at this picture. The one on the left is named Lewis. The one on the right is named Clark. Our art teacher, Ms. C., gave us paint and brushes. See how we painted each tail to tell them apart? Lewis is blue, and Clark is red. We want you to know all about our new pets, so visit this blog again soon!

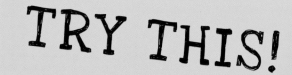

TRY THIS!

Now comes the fun part! Brainstorm some possible titles for your first blog post and make a list of what you might say. Then write away!

To get a copy of this activity, visit www.cherrylakepublishing.com/activities.

Which of the following would be okay to mention online, and which should be kept private? Discuss them with a parent or teacher if you are unsure.

- Your first name
- The name of your pet
- Your last name
- What TV shows you like to watch
- Your school's name
- Your teacher's name
- What you saw when you went to New York City
- Your address
- Your e-mail address
- Your phone number

CHAPTER FOUR
Working with Blog Comments

Comments are a great way to share your ideas with a blog's author.

Have you ever been asked to read someone's writing in class and write a message at the bottom? If so, then that message you left was a **comment**. Blogs are usually set up for readers to leave comments as well. This can help your blog become a conversation between you and your readers. It is fun to leave comments on your friends' and classmates' blogs. Here are a few things to keep in mind:

- *Be **polite**.* Remember that real people will read your comments. If you type something rude, you could hurt the author's feelings. The best strategy is to always be polite, both offline and online. Polite comments make the writer feel appreciated. Try a comment like, "This post helped me really imagine how big the Grand Canyon is!" If you have a suggestion, word it politely. For example, "Next time you post, could you tell us more about the concession stand?" That sounds more appealing than, "Hey, you didn't talk about the concession stand!" One makes the writer want to help you, and the other does not!

Be careful what you post in blog comments. Blog authors and other readers will all be able to see what you write.

- *Be **helpful**.* If you have suggestions for improvement, explain them clearly and respectfully. Would you like to hear, "This post stinks!" (not helpful)? Or would you rather hear, "Next time, I hope you will tell us more about what happened when you got a flat tire" (helpful)?

- *Be **specific**.* The more detail you can give, the better. That's true even with compliments, which everyone loves! A comment like "Great post" is nice. But it doesn't tell the writer very much about why you liked it. Here's a more specific comment: "Wow, your story about how the hamsters chewed through the toilet paper tubes overnight was so funny!" This lets the writer know exactly what he or she did well.

Good comments help bloggers improve their writing in future blog posts.

TRY THIS!

You be the judge! Which of the following comments are helpful, polite, or specific? Which are not?

- Try harder next time.
- Your description of the hamsters' nest used great adjectives.
- I loved when you told about the bus trip to the state capitol. I could feel your excitement!
- Nice try, but no good.

- What makes you think you're a good blogger?
- I have no idea what you're talking about.
- Next time, please tell us more about the food fight in the cafeteria. Did food get on your clothes?

To get a copy of this activity, visit www.cherrylakepublishing.com/activities

CHAPTER FIVE

Reading Other People's Blogs with RSS

RSS feeds help you stay up to date with all of your favorite blogs.

You and your friends have now set up blogs. How will you know when your fellow bloggers have written something new? You could type in the URLs of your favorite blogs every day. But you might check six days in a row without seeing any updates, or new posts. That takes up a lot of time.

Wouldn't it be great if you could go to one place and see all of your friends' new posts at once? You can do that with a tool that supports **RSS**.

RSS stands for Really Simple Syndication. That sounds complicated, but RSS is actually really easy. If you use it, you won't have to visit each of your friends' blogs to check for updates. Those updates are delivered to you as soon as your friends post them! RSS is kind of like the post office. It sends you mail so you don't have to pick it up!

To follow blogs with RSS, you need to use an **aggregator**. An aggregator is a special kind of Web site. You set up an account and tell the site which blogs you want to follow. Some popular RSS aggregators include iGoogle and Google Reader. Each of them looks a bit different. Choose whichever one you like best.

After you set up your account, you'll need to tell the aggregator which blogs you want to follow. Find the button that asks you to add a **subscription** or a **feed**. Paste in the URL of one of your friend's blogs. Now you're set up! The next time you log in to your aggregator account, it will quickly check your friend's blog. If there's something new, it will be delivered right to your screen.

Now you and your friends know how to safely set up, write, and read blogs. All that's left is for you to think of exciting new things to post!

What will you blog about next?

TRY THIS!

RSS aggregators such as iGoogle and Google Reader both have their own advantages. Try iGoogle if you want to set up a custom Web page with RSS included. Try Google Reader if you just want to check RSS feeds.

To get a copy of this activity, visit www.cherrylakepublishing.com/activities.

Add a subscription to your friends' blogs. You can also find subscriptions for lots of other online Web sites that aren't blogs. For example, you can subscribe to Sports Illustrated, your local newspaper, comics sites, and more.

In the future, when you're browsing the Web, keep your eyes open for these logos. They are a sign that you can read the site through your aggregator!

UPDATE UPDATE

RSS

Glossary

aggregator (AG-ruh-gay-tur) an online tool that gathers new posts and content from your favorite blogs and Web sites and delivers them to a single place online

blog (BLAWG) a special kind of Web site where you can easily add new information whenever you want

body (BAH-dee) the main area of a blog post, where you write your paragraphs or share text, audio, photos, or video

comment (CAH-ment) a reader's written response to a blog post

customize (KUHS-tuh-mize) change something to suit your needs

feed (FEED) a word to describe your blog content as it is delivered to an aggregator via RSS

posts (POHSTS) individual entries in a blog

RSS (AR ESS ESS) Really Simple Syndication: online coding that helps an aggregator pull content from a blog or Web site

subscription (sub-SCRIP-shun) an arrangement to receive updates from an RSS feed

templates (TEM-plits) premade layouts for your blog that include the frame of colors, images, and designs that surround your blog posts

text (TEKST) words

URL (YOO AR EL) stands for Universal Resource Locator, a fancy of way of saying "Web address"

Web hosts (WEB HOSTS) companies that you can pay to get your own Web site; they store your content and make it available to the public

Find Out More

BOOKS

Cornwall, Phyllis. *Online Etiquette and Safety*. Ann Arbor, MI: Cherry Lake, 2011.

Hile, Lori. *Social Networks and Blogs*. Chicago: Raintree, 2011.

Mack, James. *Journals and Blogging*. Chicago: Raintree, 2009.

Raatma, Lucia. *Blogs*. Ann Arbor, MI: Cherry Lake, 2010.

WEB SITES

The Edublog Awards Blog

http://edublogawards.com

Find award-winning blogs in the Best Student Blog category and get inspired!

Mrs. Yollis' Classroom Blog

http://yollisclassblog.blogspot.com

Visit Mrs. Yollis' third-grade class online. This blog won the Edublog Award for Best Class Blog in 2011. You can see the class blog and link to students' individual blogs.

Index

About the Author

Kristin Fontichiaro teaches at the University of Michigan. She has been blogging for more than five years.